Be That Cloud

Cloud

By Kat Louise

ISBN: 9798844013775 (paperback)

ISBN: 9798847839334 (hardback)

Acknowledgements

Thanks to my dear friends and children, who believe in me. In particular, to my best friend, for making me realise my potential and making it happen.

X

Introduction

We live in an unpredictable world, where we are striving for happiness, reaching for that goal as well as recovering from set-backs. Often, many of us will sit and over-analyse our thinking and be afraid to seek support, as we know others are going through the same (we do not want to be seen as a burden). I cannot emphasise enough the reasons to move forwards, with more self- belief and the ability to reach out, as well as validate your purpose in life. We need to look after our mental health and be less judgmental, as we never know what is happening in anyone's lives. Many find it hard to process their thinking, move on/manage feelings in life, and deal with heart ache and loss. Often, there is just an empty feeling that cannot be explained.

Positivity and strength are being sent to all those who need it. Do take time to reflect after reading these poems, as they are written from many perspectives, of which you may relate to. You are not alone on this journey. Reach out, speak out.

Kat Louise

x

Contents

Acceptance

For who is one to judge?

Compare me not, for there is only one of me

In a forever changing world, accept my difference

What lies beneath is the same, you and I

Unique in my own rights

Individuality lies here and may expanse into
yonder

Dark Shadow

The dark shadow of the past lingers

Forbidden to encroach on the now

Take a positive step forwards and release
uncertainties

You are worth so much more

The dark shadow has been betrayed

You have faith and confidence, you have let go

Accept nothing but kindness and love

For you deserve so much more

Choices

I thought it was my time

Yet something sat heavy on my chest, I cannot
explain

To find the one I had been waiting for

Longing for acceptance and understanding

My mind will not sleep

Spinning like a top, caught in a whirlwind of fear

I can only hope the heaviness will ease

Right choices need to be made

Rest

Now my friend, take time

For you cannot forever burn bright

The greatest smiles can wane like the moonlight

Listen to the cool breeze brushing your soft skin

Feel what you feel, no need to hide

Unlock those precious thoughts and rest

When you are ready, you may light the candle
once again

Worry Not

I wake in fear, eyes bright

My heart thumps like a pendulum ticking

Those vivid images race through my exhausted
brain

Worry not, for it has not happened

The fear and confusion take hold

Racing rapidly, calm words needed

I return to my cold pillow

Worry not, for it has not happened

Take a Chance

It is waiting for you, yet there is darkened fear
creeping back

Make that giant leap of faith and stay focused

Burst through those barriers

Let it happen

Take a chance

Be Proud

You have come so far

The tiniest of steps will add to a multitude of new
beginnings

Let the door open wide to new opportunities

As the wilted flower begins to grow

Take a deep breath and believe

For only YOU will make this happen

Learn to trust yourself again and be proud

Today and always

Goals

Free the self-doubt as you can achieve those
goals

Contentment should be worn with pride

Not sat silently in your shadow

Kindness

Be kind to yourself

As the realisation of time has become more
apparent

Have more self-compassion and take kindly to
your mistakes

Share your light and forgive

Go beyond those impossible dreams and be that
someone of great worth

Be that anchor to others

Let the inner-glow radiate, for the world needs to
see your light

My Shadow

A mysterious shadow surrounds me

An ambience, stirring enchanting thoughts

For who is the shadow sending strength and encouragement?

Overcome with emotion, I lay upon the dewy grass

Teardrops run free, as the wind sings my name

Lost

As my heart bleeds

The solitude leads to confusion

Shattered fragments of my mind feel like poison

Whisper to me

Guide me

For I am lost

Smile

Sometimes we forget to smile

We judge those who don't

Do we know what is hiding?

No...

Often, a mountain of worries pulling on
heartstrings

Maybe lonely souls, a smile once a distant
memory

Lift others and share yours

Even if they hold onto it for that short moment

Hold On

Belief is not beyond my grasp

As I see the golden sunlight emerge from the
distance

My mind feels warm and accepting

There is hope, as positivity surrounds my once,
darkened soul

I will take this moment and hold it tight

For I shall not return

I will embrace the now

I am ready

My Younger Self

Sitting silently, calmly

Feeling the warmth on my bare skin

I catch a glimpse of my former self

The innocence and vulnerabilities

Heartache and laughter

Wishing to be that older self

Hold on to some of those beautiful memories
and wrap them up tight

Set others free…

Memories can never be erased or re-written

So live for the now

My Mind

A whirlwind of vivid colours screams through the night

All I want is calm

Grey, deepening to the darkest embers

The rapid roller coaster is still alive

Twisting and turning

When will it stop?

Hibernation is Over

As we move away from those darkened days

Destiny awaits

A never-ending lustrous rainbow of happiness no longer sleeps

Now stirring by the new-found self

The brightened palette's brilliance is apparent

Sunshine

Be that light dancing on the water

Rejoice and stand proud

Be fearless, controlling your destiny

Smile bright

Create your own sunshine

Be That Cloud

Find a moment to be still

Watching the candy-floss filled sky

As the feathery clouds sail on by

Each unique

A forever-changing cycle of tranquillity

As the sunlight casts a lazy hue

They take their place

Be that cloud

Live the Dream

There's fulfilment if we make it happen

Endless possibilities surround you

Hold onto that dream with optimism

Do not let it slip, under the pillow's spell

Let the conscious mind thrive

Live those etched thoughts of contentment

For they shall not sleep

I Can

My mind forbids me to give up

As the voice inside shares the commitment to
succeed

I will stand proud in pursuit of that goal

Having the strength to achieve

My soul will guide me

With the inner-strength and fearlessness take
hold

Yet

What stops you?

The voices hurt

They said you never could

A mind full of self-doubt

Mirrored negativities

The voice will change

You can

Maybe not now

Not yet

Future

As the sweet aroma of spring fills the air

The iridescent moon shines

Clear skies open the blanket of glistening stars

Who are we to say what the future may hold?

Time

Every precious moment

The clock ticks

Do not wait for tomorrow

Live each day as your last

Sit silently

Laugh loudly

Love and be loved

Be kind

No time for regrets

Move forwards

For it'll be gone...

Blossom

Let the light of day embrace the infinite journey

May warmth calm the mind

A soft breeze will blow those tussled locks

Unfold those rigid fingers

Stand tall and smell the sweet nectar

As you blossom and grow

Unite

Shall the way I look define me?

When what lies beneath is the same

How can the greed of one's soul destroy the
innocent?

When peace and unity is what we strive for

Stand together and share harmony, in the face of
adversity.

I Am Enough

I shall not compare

As the outer beauty will forever be untold

Why does the outer shell be judged?

I strive to be the best and have been beaten

If only we could visualise the beauty of one's soul
through the eyes

Looks may fade yet my heart will remain

For I am enough

Take My Hand

Walk with me

Feel the warmth of the sun unite our souls

Place your hand in mine sharing sweet memories

I know you guide me daily, missed sorely

We have laughed, we have loved

Take my hand for now

What If?

What if the world started being kind?

What if we smiled at a stranger?

What if we stopped comparing our lives?

What if…

What if we said thanks more often?

What if we could say sorry?

What if we could stop and listen and be heard?

What if…

A New Day Dawns

Once empty with no direction

Pain, not wanting for tomorrow

Learning to blossom and grow

Seeking warmth, love and tranquillity

Like the golden sunrise emerging from beyond
the smiling seas

There is a tomorrow where I will heal and grow

As a new day dawns, there is hope

Love

Hugs that heal

I feel safe

Eyes sparkle with no words needed

The warm breadth brushes my skin

Imperfections in my mind have faded

As many stories are told and memories made

I am wanted, loved, not needed

The Eyes Speak

The language of the soul

Not written, not spoken

Lies deep as the eyes speak

No prompting, no arguments

Revealing what the heart conceals

Friendship

Stand by my side beautiful friend

Share the joys and pain with unconditional love

Laugh uncontrollably, endlessly

As tears roll down our flushed cheeks

Let stories be told without judgement

Always and forever

Belief

It is not beyond my tightened grasp

As my mind has calmed and more accepting

A once broken soul is mending

As the positivity makes the spine tingle

I see beyond the misty waters

I am ready

Twisted Roots

Wherever the roots may have once belonged

You may never always belong to that same tree

Entwined, often with confusion and sorrow

Find the roots from the hardy evergreen

For they will stay true to you

I Have Learned

An energetic life full of fond memories

Laughing endlessly, soul searching and tears

Love and laughter have filled the empty cup

For my path has led me to forever changing
destinations

Not a final end to the journey

I have learned, yet there is a long road ahead

Horizon

What lies beyond?

As the soft breeze whispers

Rolling hills of emerald green blankets shimmer

The burnt amber reflects off the lapping ocean

My thoughts are still as the calmness warms my
heart

As I seek comfort beyond the horizon

Don't Hold Back

The powerful desire to learn again is now

Enter a world of the unknown and take risks

Fear not, for you shall embrace new
opportunities life brings

Turn those fragile frowns the right way up

Be as free as a songbird, singing sweetly

As we know not of the universe's path

Achieve the impossible while not inhibiting your
aspirations

Jigsaw

Once the pieces did not fit

Pushed aside with a melancholy sigh

Feeling knotted, like wool from a playful kitten

Now sitting snuggly side by side

Feeling complete

Let It Go

Free yourself of the internalising thoughts

Find a place of contentment to clear the abstract
mind

The multitude of worries can be let go

They are not wanted anymore

Rainbow

Scarlett cheeks glow with pride

The day is golden

Dancing daffodils smile again

Emerald hills lead me to hope

My mind clears, like the fluffy clouds dissipating
in the royal sky above

May the amethyst protect me and support my
analytical mind

As the aromatic lavender keeps me at peace

I Fly Free

When the heavy chains have been lifted from my
damaged wings

I see the light shine like mirrored pearls

The essence of sweet cherry blossom fills the air

Contentment hits

I fly free of the hurt with a new sense of freedom

Shine

You are a blank sky, covered with shiny
diamonds

An infinite glow radiates from within

Let the inner peace remind you of your worth

Your beauty and belonging

Fill your cup with happiness and shine bright

When I Grow Up

When I grow up, I will look back and treasure the memories locked in my head

The past cannot be re-written, but I will have learned

When I would've fallen, the weary sails would've been dusted off and the fear shaken

I will be able to laugh from the un told stories

For I will have lived and learned

However, many more stories are to be made…

Be Kind to Yourself

Take your mind to a calm land

Where the sea whispers kindness and peace

Listen to the negativity of the inner-voice

As perfection ceases to exist

Share your desires, expressions and truth

Capabilities are endless

Enlighten the power within you and be kind

Mistakes

My best teacher is my last mistake

Why do I forever celebrate the successes?

When I should unpick the falsity and
misjudgements

I shall seize the moment and master what has
been learned

I will move forward with my new-found wisdom

And flourish

Breathe

I will stop being the ultimate hero and say no

Just for now, taking a calm and steady breath

Releasing the anguish deep from within

I will breathe out the positivity and happiness and
relinquish the desire to control my future,

For I am here in the present

The Storm

As the passionate distemper materialises

My tongue shall stay silent, taught with
frustration

The fierceness is an unstoppable force

My burning desire to stand one's ground remains
hesitant

All I want is harmony with the storm subsiding

Undisturbed

Still

Take Time to Heal

After heartache and pain, where a cold silence
freezes the soul,

Take time to heal

When emptiness tears you down, with a sense of
disconnection,

Take time to heal

As life moves on, immense pressure will build
wanting you to blossom and grow,

Take time to heal

I Sense Happiness

Catch a falling star and make that wish

Sing freely, as you dance daintily though the
sunlit fields

Join the playful raindrops as they dance in unison

Hug the freedom of now

Breaking the habitual habit of doom

Embracing the new self, smelling sweet scents of
what tomorrow may bring

Shiny Pebble

Where lies the shiny pebble?

For which the crashing waves have cleansed

Once unnoticed, not displaying its inner beauty

Now its prominence apparent and true-self

Peeking through the wisps of the sea mist

Polished and proud

A Promise to Myself

From today, each step will be filled with positivity
and forgiveness

I endeavour to live in peace and harmony

Endless worries shall not be trapped inside my
puzzled mind

Others will be listened to with an open heart

I will ease myself into more joyous times where
possible

As the universe may at times, play its
unpredictable card

The Next Chapter

Life is full of forever changing chapters

As the pages are turned, some unfinished

Others torn and ripped out, forgotten

Entangled, I have often felt in my dewy web

For now, as the next page turns I will go beyond
what sits comfortably

Uncertainties that have once surrounded me will
make me stronger and believe the impossible
dream

I will strive to be that better me

I will look after myself and understand my
purpose

My new Chapter awaits...

Final note

Look after yourselves. Seek help when needed, as well as supporting those in need and be kind. We have one life, so live it and cherish every living moment. Be the best you can be and thrive!

X

Be that cloud…

Useful links for support:

www.mind.org.uk

www.samaritans.org

www.nhs.uk/nhs-services/mental-health-services

www.rethink.org

www.giveusashout.org

Printed in Great Britain
by Amazon

12717809R00068